Davy Crockett

YOUNG PIONEER

Davy Crockett

YOUNG PIONEER

by Laurence Santrey
illustrated by Francis Livingston

Troll Associates

Library of Congress Cataloging in Publication Data

Santrey, Laurence.
    Davy Crockett, young pioneer.

    Summary: Profiles the childhood of Davy Crockett,
pioneer and patriot.
    1. Crockett, Davy, 1786-1836—Juvenile literature.
2. Pioneers—Tennessee—Juvenile literature.
3. Tennessee—Biography—Juvenile literature.
4. Legislators—United States—Biography—Juvenile
literature.   5. United States. Congress. House—
Biography—Juvenile literature.   [1. Crockett, Davy,
1786-1836.   2. Pioneers.   3. Legislators]   I. Livingston, Francis, ill.   II. Title.
F436.C95S26   1983   976.8 '04 '0924   [B]   [92]   82-16040
ISBN 0-89375-847-7
ISBN 0-89375-848-5 (pbk.)

Davy Crockett

YOUNG PIONEER

"Pa! Pa!" The little boy burst into the cabin. "There's a big bear out in the woods," he cried. "It saw me, but I got away. It's out there right now!"

"Calm down, Davy," said the boy's father. "Just where did you see this bear?"

"Down by the bend in the stream, near that big patch of huckleberries." The words tumbled out of Davy's mouth.

"That's about a mile from here," John Crockett said, staring hard at his four-year-old son. Then he took his long rifle from the rack on the wall.

"Can I come with you, Pa?" Davy begged. "I can take you to the spot where I saw the bear."

"You stay right here, David Crockett!" Mrs. Crockett commanded. "Your father will go after the bear. Then, when he returns, I think he'll want to have a word or two with you."

Rebecca Crockett took the boy by the hand and sat him down on a wooden stool next to the big fireplace.

"Oh, Ma," Davy wailed. "You and Pa never let me do anything. My brothers can go anywhere they want in the woods. They have all the fun. It's not fair."

The dark-haired woman smiled. "Well, Davy, they're all older than you. Young Johnny is thirteen, you know—almost a man. And James —he's eleven and does a full day's chores with your Pa. William and Wilson don't wander, and they're both older than you. Instead of running off into the woods, why don't you help me take care of the little ones?"

"I don't want to take care of babies," said Davy. "I want to hunt and fish. I want to have my own rifle so that I can hunt."

"There'll be plenty of time for that when you're big enough to hold a rifle," Mrs. Crockett said gently.

When John Crockett returned to the cabin, it was almost dark. But he was smiling. "Rebecca," he said, standing at the door, "I've brought you a fine bearskin cover for the bed and plenty of meat for the family. That bear was a fat one!"

"Good. We can use the fat to make soap and candles," Mrs. Crockett answered. "I'm very happy you got that bear."

"Are you happy I found it for you?" Davy piped up.

"I'm pleased you found it, son," Mr. Crockett said. "And I thank you for that. But I'm not very happy that you found it down by the stream, because that means you were where you shouldn't have been. And you know what that means."

Davy sighed, for he knew it meant a spanking. He didn't like that one bit, but he accepted his punishment with only a few sniffles. Mr. Crockett was a strict, but fair man. All the Crockett children were taught never to go off alone into the woods. The year was 1790, and there were many dangerous wild animals in the Tennessee territory where they lived.

After the spanking, Davy's parents made him promise not to go off into the woods without at least one of his big brothers. Davy wasn't happy about it, but he obeyed the order. The older Crockett boys didn't like it any better. It was no fun to have their little brother tagging along with them everywhere they went.

One day, the Crockett boys and a teenage friend named Campbell were playing near the Nolichucky River. All of the older boys got into Mr. Crockett's canoe, leaving Davy on the shore. The four-year-old boy didn't like that at all, but there wasn't a thing he could do about it. So he sat on the ground and watched. Davy never forgot what happened next:

"My brothers had been used to paddling the canoe and could have taken it safely anywhere around there. But this fellow Campbell wouldn't let them have the paddle. Instead, like a fool, he tried to manage the canoe himself.

"I guess he had never been in a canoe before, because it went any way but the way he wanted it to go. He paddled, and paddled, and paddled —all the while going the wrong way. In a short time, they were going backward toward the falls."

Little Davy, furious that he was missing the excitement of the wild canoe ride, began to jump up and down, screaming loudly. A farmer, working in a nearby field, heard the noise and came running. The man saw the canoe heading for the falls, and he dived into the water to rescue the boys. By the time he reached them, they were no more than a few feet from the edge. The farmer lunged forward, gripping the side of the canoe with both hands.

"He hung on to the canoe till he got it stopped, and then drew it out of danger," Davy remembered. "When they got out, I found the boys were more scared than I had been. And the only thing that comforted me was the belief that it was their punishment for leaving me on shore."

Davy's young life was filled with adventure. When he was six years old, his uncle, Joseph Hawkins, took him out hunting. Davy had pleaded with the grownups to teach him how to track animals in the woods and how to shoot.

Now, even though the rifle was bigger than Davy,
Uncle Joe agreed to give him hunting lessons.

The tall man in buckskin quietly led the way
through the woods. Davy followed closely,
trying to be just as quiet. Every now and then
Uncle Joe paused, held up a hand to signal Davy
to stay still, and listened.

"A good woodsman," he told Davy, "can hear a deer or a bear or a wildcat, even when it's far off in the woods. In fact, a good woodsman uses *all* his senses. Sometimes he can hear things he can't see. Sometimes he can see an animal, or signs that take him to it. And sometimes he can smell the critter when he can't see or hear it."

Together, Davy and his Uncle Joe spent many afternoons tracking deer, bear, and other game. Their adventures often led across small streams, past oaks and hickories and sassafras trees. The hours would quickly pass, as they tramped along through the underbrush. Davy loved these outings. He found there was always something new to learn about the animals and plants of the forest. And Davy knew he was lucky to have such a fine woodsman to teach him.

When Davy was almost eight years old, the Crocketts moved to Cove Creek, Tennessee, where Mr. Crockett bought a piece of land right next to the creek. He told the family that this was a perfect place for a mill.

Davy's father and older brothers started to work right away. They had to make the water wheel, set up the grindstone, and build the family's living quarters over the millhouse. John Crockett had great hopes for making a success of the mill. There was a steady flow of settlers into the area, and they would all need a place to take their grain to be ground into flour.

There was plenty of work to do at the Crocketts' place, but not for someone as young as Davy. Anyway, he wasn't very interested in learning to build. His heart was set on hunting. Every day, he asked his father and his older brothers to take him into the forest. But they were always too busy. At last, Mr. Crockett told Davy to take the rifle and go hunting by himself. But Mr. Crockett had one condition. Because bullets were expensive, the boy was given just one bullet a day. Mr. Crockett told him to use it carefully.

21

"Hunting is a serious thing, Davy," his father said. "We don't shoot for fun. We do it for the food and the skins. So, before you pull the trigger, make sure you aren't going to waste that bullet."

For the first few days, the young hunter came home empty-handed. He made too much noise and scared off the animals. He shot too fast, afraid he would miss his chance. Or he waited too long, and the animal picked up his scent. But after a while, Davy started to make his bullets count. Then, the Crockett family had meat for dinner almost every night.

Years later, when Davy was asked how he came to be such a great hunter and crack shot, he had a simple answer. He explained that, because his father had given him just one bullet a day, he *had* to learn to be smart and patient. "Add to that a sharp eye and a good rifle," he would say, "and you're a hunter."

24

Winter passed, and in March the mill was finished. The spring rains came soon after, swelling the creek and turning the water wheel quickly. This pleased the Crocketts. But the rains didn't stop. The creek water rose higher and higher, flooding the mill. Soon, the water reached the second floor, where the family lived. The Crocketts had to get out of the house and head for high ground.

When the creek was back to normal, the family returned to their house. It had been totally wrecked. The big water wheel had been swept away. The huge grindstone was cracked, and the house itself was in terrible shape. Gathering everything that was worth saving, the Crocketts left Cove Creek forever.

25

Davy's next home was an inn his father decided to buy. It was next to a road that went from Abingdon, Virginia to Knoxville, Tennessee. Hunters, trappers, settlers, and other travelers passed this way. It was a small country inn, with room enough for the family and a few paying guests.

Mrs. Crockett did the cooking and took care of the younger children. Mr. Crockett and the older children served the guests, fed and stabled their horses, and raised vegetables behind the inn. Davy, who at nine years old was a sure-eyed hunter, had the job of bringing home meat for the table. The Crocketts lived this way for the next three years.

When Davy was twelve, a farmer by the name of Jacob Siler stopped at the inn on his way from Tennessee to Virginia. He had with him a wagon, a team of horses, and a herd of cattle. During dinner, Mr. Siler complained to Mr. Crockett that he was finding it difficult to manage the horses and the cattle himself. He asked if one of the Crockett boys would be able to travel with him. Mr. Siler was ready to pay the boy a fair wage. Mr. Crockett thought about it for a moment, then asked Davy if he would like to go. The boy, always ready for a new adventure, thought it was a wonderful idea.

The next morning, Mr. Siler and Davy set out on the 400-mile trip to Virginia. Davy walked every step of the way, keeping the cattle from straying or getting lost. When he reached the Virginia farm, Davy received five dollars. Then Mr. Siler told Davy he wanted him to stay on the farm as a hired hand. Davy really wanted to go home, but he remembered Mr. Crockett's last words to him: "Obey Mr. Siler." Although the boy was very homesick, he wanted to do what his father had told him to do. He stayed.

A few weeks later, while Davy was walking along the road near the farm, he met Mr. Dunn, a neighbor from Tennessee. Dunn and his two sons were driving three wagons loaded with goods they had bought in Virginia. Davy told the man what he was doing there, how much he missed his family, and that he wanted to go home. After Mr. Dunn heard the whole story, he assured Davy that it would be all right for him to go back to Tennessee. Even so, Davy was scared to tell Mr. Siler he was leaving. He decided he would have to sneak away from the farm.

"We're staying at the inn seven miles down this road," Mr. Dunn told Davy. "We'll be leaving for Tennessee at sun-up tomorrow. If you get there by then, I'll be pleased to take you home."

Davy went back to the Siler farm. He gathered his clothes and what little money he had. Then he went to bed. But his eagerness to begin the trip home was too great, and he could not sleep.

About three hours before sunrise, Davy left the Siler farm. Snow was falling heavily, and nearly eight inches of the white powder already covered the ground. There was no moon to light the way, for the falling snow filled the night sky. Davy had to guess his way along the road that led to the inn.

By the time Davy reached Mr. Dunn's wagon, the snow was as high as his knees and there was still an hour before daybreak. He had walked seven miles in deep snow and total darkness in just two hours! He was exhausted and almost frozen stiff—but he couldn't have been happier. Mr. Dunn welcomed the boy, got him some breakfast, and sent him to warm himself by the fire. A short while later, the Dunns, their three wagons,

and Davy set out on their journey to Tennessee.

The Crocketts were as delighted to see Davy as he was to be back home. But another adventure awaited Davy, who had just turned thirteen. A man named Benjamin Kitchen had opened a little country school down the road from the Crockett house. Mr. Crockett decided his children should get some education—the first schooling for any of them.

Davy went to school for four days. In that time, he began to learn to read and write the alphabet. Then, on the afternoon of the fourth day, Davy got into a fight on the way home from school. It was with a classmate who had been making fun of Davy. After the fight, which Davy won, he knew he was in deep trouble. Mr. Kitchen didn't like fighting, and he threatened to whip any children who used their fists. Davy did not want a whipping.

The next morning, when the Crockett boys left for school, Davy went only part of the way with them. After his brothers promised not to tell their father, he spent the day in the woods. He continued to do this for several days. Finally, Mr. Kitchen sent a note to Mr. Crockett, asking why Davy had been absent.

Mr. Crockett had a talk with Davy. When he learned why the boy was playing hooky, Mr. Crockett said, "Make your choice, Davy. If you go to school, you'll get a whipping from your teacher. If you don't go, you'll get a worse one from me."

Davy didn't like the choice at all. He felt the best thing to do was to run off for a little while, until his father and Mr. Kitchen had a chance to cool down. He took a job with a man who was driving a herd of cattle to Virginia. When they got to the end of the trail, Davy was paid four dollars and told he was on his own.

At this point, Davy wanted to go home, but he couldn't. First, a wagoner promised to take him to Tennessee, but changed his mind. Then Davy's money was stolen, and he had to find a job. He could have risked walking the hundreds of miles back home, but he had no money to buy food along the way.

Instead, Davy worked at one job after another for almost three years. He was a plow-boy on a farm, an apprentice to a hat maker, a wagoner's helper, and a clean-up boy in a mill. At last, in the spring of 1802, Davy met a man willing to take him on his wagon to Tennessee. Davy was going home.

One evening, Davy, now tall, broad-shouldered, and looking very grown up, walked into the Crocketts' inn. He did not identify himself. Instead, he behaved like a guest.

As Davy remembered many years after, "I had been gone so long, and had grown so much, that the family did not at first know me. After a while, all the guests were called to supper. I went with the rest. We sat down to the table and began to eat, when my eldest sister recognized me. She sprang up, ran and seized me around the neck, and exclaimed, 'Here is my lost brother!'"

The family was so glad to see Davy again that he regretted having stayed away so long. When he found out how much they had missed him, he wished he had taken his whipping and gone back to school. But the time spent away from home had not been wasted. Davy had learned a lot about life, about right and wrong, and about what it meant to be grown up.

Davy had a chance to prove this right away. Mr. Crockett owed thirty-six dollars to Abraham Wilson, a local farmer. Davy offered to work for the man, to pay off the debt. It took him six months of hard work, but he stuck with it. The teenager was very proud on the day he gave his father the piece of paper that declared the debt paid in full. A short while later, Davy went to work for a man named John Kennedy, to pay off another family debt. It took the young man six more months to clear up that forty-dollar debt.

In the summer of 1803, Davy hired out to work again—for himself. It was on the farm of a local schoolteacher. In place of money as payment, the teenager asked for food, a place to stay, and schooling. In the next six months, the teacher taught Davy to read, write, and do some arithmetic. That was all the formal education Davy ever had, but he felt it was the best payment he ever received for his work.

Now Davy Crockett was a man in his own right, and a very able one, too. As a woodsman, he had no equal in the whole state of Tennessee. He could track any animal, and with old Betsy, his trusty rifle, he brought down many a bear, cougar, wildcat, and deer. Word of Davy's skill spread, and the legends that grew around him soon became part of America's folklore. One legend tells how Davy killed 105 bears in one year. Another claims he tamed a huge alligator. There is no end to the tall tales about the amazing Davy Crockett.

His fame grew even greater as a scout under General Andrew Jackson in the War of 1812, as an officer in the citizens' army of Tennessee, and then as a member of the United States Congress. But Davy Crockett's greatest fame—and finest moment—came for his part in the heroic defense of the Alamo, a small fort in San Antonio, Texas. There, a small band of soldiers fought a gallant battle for the independence of Texas. They held out as long as they could before being overrun by a huge army of Mexicans led by General Santa Anna.

On March 6, 1836, the great pioneer and patriot died along with the other brave defenders of the Alamo. He was only forty-nine years old. But in his short lifetime, Davy Crockett carved a legend of skill and courage that will live forever.